Notes I Write to Myself in My Sleep

poems by Bruce Famoly

Clare Songbirds Publishing House Poetry Series
ISBN 978-1-947653-38-2
Clare Songbirds Publishing House
Notes I Write to Myself in My Sleep© 2018 Bruce Famoly
All Rights Reserved. Clare Songbirds Publishing House retains right to reprint.
Permission to reprint individual poems must be obtained from the author who owns the copyright.

Printed in the United States of America
FIRST EDITION

Clare Songbirds Publishing House Mission Statement:
Clare Songbirds Publishing House was established to provide a print forum for the creation of limited edition, fine art from poets and writers, both established and emerging. We strive to reignite and continue a tradition of quality, accessible literary arts to the national and international community of writers, and readers. Chapbook manuscripts are carefully chosen for their ability to propel the expansion of art and ideas in literary form. We provide an accessible way to promote the art of words in order to resonate with, and impact, readers not yet familiar with the siren song of poets and writers. Clare Songbirds Publishing House espouses a singular cultural development where poetry creates community and becomes commonplace in public places.

140 Cottage Street
Auburn, New York 13021
www.claresongbirdspub.com

Contents

Can't Sleep	7
Why?	8
How?	9
And	10
Healing Wings	11
Just Go	12
Raining Desires	13
My Soliloquy	14
neither	16
A Love	17
Rambunctious On A One Way Street	18
Yawn	19
One	20
You Faded	21
As Cloudy Beer	22
He Walks Alone	23
rejection	24
Being Me	25
She Appeared	26
I Have Had It	27
My Heart	28
Alone	29
My Message To Love	30
Part of You	31
peace	32
star	33
Electric	34
I'll Be The Judge	35
Compare	36
Frustrations	37
Yes	38
What Are You Looking At?	39
Can You Tell Me?	40
The Machine	41
Temptress	42
That Glance	44
I Watched You Dance	45
It All Came To Me	46
It's Out There	48
Accepted, Loved, Liked	49
Did You Ever?	50
The More You Don't Know	51
Museum	52

I Know I Read It	53
Astride This Horse	54
Around The Table	55
Trail Of Dreams	56
Damage Report	57
I Need To Believe	58
Perhaps	59
And Still I Wonder	60
Drifting	62
Empty	63
Bound With Blue	64
A Rush	65
It Is Deafening	66
Recycle	67
Beanstalks	68
Shoes	69
Man In The Window	70
The Box	72
Midnight On The Water	73

This collection of poems is dedicated to two wonderful women, Pam Gordon and Linda Doyle. Their kind, gentle persistence taught me that dreams and books can come true!

Can't Sleep

Holding her so tightly, so tightly
She asks, why?
A tear in my eye as I answer
Because this is where I belong
This is where I feel safe
This is where it makes sense
In the darkness I feel her smile
Her fingers trace a gentle pattern on my cheek
She whispers
Don't ever let go
Suddenly aware of the glow of the bedside clock
Wondering
Did this ever happen?
Will it ever happen to me?
Turning on the late night news
Can't sleep

Why?

Why does this old desk feel so comfortable?
Oh!
I see it now
It's where I have poured out my heart
My heart touches everything on here
Everything on here touches my heart
The tools with which I have written my life
Why does this old desk feel so comfortable?
Oh! I see them now
The tiny stains of a million tears
Please
Don't be sad for me
These stains mean that I am alive
Feeling
Remembering
Reliving
Rejoicing
Why does this old desk feel so comfortable?
Oh!
I see it now
It's where I am truly me

How

how
how do I say I love you
without saying
I love you
how
how do I keep hoping
without hoping
you love me
how
how do I come to that place
where I realize
hope is lost
how
how do I face you
without facing the fact
that you don't love me
how
how do I convince myself
to move on
to stop asking how
how?

And

and the sun said
come closer
stay
i'll not hurt you
i burned
and the rain said
come closer
don't run
stay
i'll not hurt you
i drowned
and you said
come closer
don't run
stay
stay
i'll not hurt you
and you left
and....

Healing Wings

I whispered to these butterflies
Please deliver this message for me
Land softly on her heart if you will
She needs a gentle touch you see

Turning them loose to fly to you
Knowing they would find their way
Praying they land with healing in their wings
And that you feel their touch this day

Just Go

just go
please
leave me, leave me
i am not in your heart
but
you fill mine completely
taking up the space i need to welcome another
ah
you laugh now
believing there will never be another
damn you
i am beginning to believe it too
just go

Raining Desires

a drop
two...three...four
a rivulet
trickle
brook
stream
river
raging river
racing uncontrolled
into the sea
carrying all that it has gathered along the way
emptying into forever
there am i
where you?

My Soliloquy

the only one
hearing me
but now
it shall be
for you to see
for
i will write
what i say
to myself aloud
yeah
neither sore ashamed
nor
boisterous proud
reminding myself
of all the bad
you know
all the damn
bad breaks i've had
ah!
but reprimanding myself
immediately
for
so many blessings
have visited me
c'mon fool
forget the worst
always remember
the blessings first
for
they will make
misery fade
even the foolish
mistakes you've made
mistakes pale in the light
of life's treasures
after all
you are a winner
by any measure

for all the love you've lost
you have gotten back
a million times in return
what you thought you lacked
so buddy boy
be on your way
get up, get going
greet this new day
so
now you know
what I say to me
glad you could read
MY SOLILOQUY

Neither

blinded by hope
i could not see
or
did i not want to?
deaf to the truth
I could not hear
or
did i not want to?
numb to the pain
i could not feel
or
did i not want to?
now
at last
i see
i hear
i feel
am i alive?
dead?
neither
and neither is the worst place to be

A Love

A love that can never be
Yet will forever be

A love so hard to see
Yet it is all I see

A love so far away
Yet burns in me today

A love that can never be
Yet will forever be

Rambunctious on a One-Way Street

Rambunctious on a one-way street
Yeah, exactly what the ride is like
Skidding, sliding, wheelies and furious feet
Like a kid on a brand-new bike

No containing the joy to be had
Hoping the journey never ends
Supplying one's own impetus makes one glad
Exhilaration to be not matched again

Coming upon the surprise destination
No more one-way street ahead
Overcome with suffocating consternation
Wishing a different street instead

Ah, but hopefully one can return
Hurry back on those furious feet
Such life changing lessons to be learned
Rambunctious on a one-way street

Yawn

I just made it up
Simply something to write
It never happened to me
Didn't keep me awake all night

How then does it enter my mind?
How are these snippets inspired?
Perhaps I will explain
Sometime when I'm not so tired

One

This rough exterior
Belies the softness within
Oh, but if I were to confess
How would I begin?

It seems I must project
In person, as it were
The gruff, tough individual
Within whom blossoms and butterflies stir

It is not that I yearn to be hard
On the contrary, it troubles me
But conditioned by trials and tribulations
It's who I cannot help be

Ah, but here at this little desk
Ink and paper nigh at hand
With each stroke of the pen
I become this other man

Yes, it seems that I am two
Yet not questioning which is best
For we two miraculously become ONE
When I lay this head to rest

You Faded

you faded
from
a bright light
to
a distant star

from
a roaring fire
to
the last glowing ember

from
a lightning strike
to
a twinkling firefly

i faded
from
basking in your glow
to
hoping for a glimpse

you faded
you are no more

As Cloudy Beer

The stratosphere's
atmosphere
as cloudy beer

Oh tis craft
cold on draft
you think me daft?

I was there
and everywhere
without a care

Last night I think
a few to drink
made me blink

The blinking eye
of this jolly guy
hid the cry

Morning in the stratosphere
the atmosphere?
As cloudy beer

He Walks Alone

He walks alone
It is a thorny land
Oh, occasionally accompanied
By a curious band
But
Usually alone
In his mind anyway
He lets them by his side
Won't let them stay
He
Doesn't necessarily
Like walking alone
Yet only tolerating little
Of their tiresome monotone
Lonely?
Yes he can be
At least in part
His mind doesn't mind
But it pricks his heart
So
Walking on steadily
Albeit on shaky ground
He protects himself
By not looking around
There
His focus remains
Steady yet grim
By chance you pass him by
Please remember me to him

Rejection

the older
the less painful
rejection
i see my faults
more clearly now
i understand
rejection
now
a sting
then
a sledgehammer blow
the older
the less painful
rejection

Being Me

is being me
good for you
or
merely good for me
is being me
what i do
or
what you see

is being me
simply who i am
or
by my choices
is being me
what i say
or other voices

is being me
what i can't
or
what i can
is being me
make me unique
or just a man

is being me
the innocent one
or
the suspect
is being me
one you can love
or
one you reject

is being me
good for you
or
merely good for me

She Appeared

she appeared
two minutes
thirty seconds
smiles
kind hello
how are you?
fine, you?
she had to go
i know her
better than some i've known all my life
she appeared
two minutes
thirty seconds

I Have Had It

I have had it
but never got it

had enough of
having none

enough is never
way too much

I am always
never the one

always early
at being late

walk away
when I should run

going forward
in reverse

above it all
under the gun

feeling alive
to deaden the pain

this is a riot
but it ain't fun

I have had it
but never got it

had enough of
having none

My Heart

I gave my heart
Immediately
It became easy
To give all I have
Ever had
You
Took all I have
Ever had
But
Not my heart
I don't miss
What I have
Ever had
I miss
My heart

Alone

daily
surrounded
strangers
aquaintances
friends
yet
alone
with my feelings
dreams
hopes
prayers
touching bodies
missing hearts
hearts need to be touched
hearts need to touch
mostly
they need to know
oh!
they need to know
if
if they don't
alone

My Message to Love

will you find me?
or
are you not looking?
i have looked for you
even found you
but
lost you
or
did you run away?
maybe
maybe
i've been blind
unable to understand you
unwilling to compromise
ignorant
will you find me?
i've changed

Part of You

part of you
better
than all of any other

I think
I think
because

I never really experienced all
of another

maybe I didn't deserve all
of another
because
obviously
I didn't deserve part of you

did I?

Peace

where?
look
into your heart
if not there
it's nowhere!

Star

as a star
bright
beautiful
shining
piercing the darkness
with
the glow of love

as a cloud
heavy
thick
a curtain
begging darkness
by
obscuring the glow

as a fool
desiring
obtaining
possessing
becoming
that cloud
why?

another star?
forever a cloud?

perhaps only the stars know
i do not

Electric

tingle
you touched my hand
exciting
inviting
shock
you said goodbye
paralyzing
debilitating
electric
this life I lead
always
a charge

I'll Be the Judge

i'm a suspect
just been informed
knew it was coming
didn't need to be warned

comin after me
knew they would
make it go away
if I could

foolish man
trying to hide
fooling myself
deny, deny

find me guilty
without fail
no need for lock up
in my own jail

Compare

compare
back ache
heart ache

can't
impossible
no comparison

therapy
straighten up
back feels better

no therapy
only time
sometimes never enough time

will I live?
Yes
no!!!

damn, I must

Frustrations

Frustrations come in many forms
Many shapes and sizes
Clearly seen and bumped into
But many in disguises

Make the hair on your neck stand up
Or knock you to your knees
Put you into heated situations
Or in a deep, deep freeze

Cruising, sailing with the wind
At once the breeze dead still
No movement now, stuck in place
A test of mind, body and will

Oh, fear not, you are not alone
Not the first, nor will you be the last
Frustrations may linger, a tenacious hold
Or come and go so fast

Part of life, part of who we are
Let me tell you sister, brother
We are increasingly missing this critical point
Frustrations are why we need each other

Yes

yes, she was there
glad
not so glad
what is beautiful
is torture
within reach
out of reach
touchable
untouchable
longing
losing
leaving
with memories
only memories
yes, she was there

What Are You Looking At

Yep, I've got bodily flaws and some scars
Don't care to hide their existence
Flaws and scars are part of who we are
Accidents and too much beer for instance

Some are hard won victory nicks
Others the result of foolish mistakes
Oh, I guess for one or two there is a fix
Not sure just what it would take

The blemishes are me, a bit of who I am
What I've been through by choice or nay
Explain each one? Not sure I can
Exactly what would you like me to say?

They are there and I am here
Not hiding even the slightest of these
You've got some too? Hell, I don't care
Let's look into each other's hearts. Please!

Can You Tell Me

can you tell me
what does the world look like
in the middle of a somersault,
on a tightrope,
in a skydive?
What does the world look like
at 200 miles per hour,
under the ocean,
from space?
Can you tell me
what does the world look like
when you're in love?
tell me please

Temptress

She tempts me
Oh
Not on purpose
She doesn't try
She doesn't have to
It's on me
My desires
Hopes
Yes, dreams
She tempts me
Not for any reason
Not to cause pain
Not for revenge
Merely
Because she exists
Because she is
She tempts me

The Machine

Adjusted, polished and thoroughly cleaned
The last bolts tightened into place
A beautiful, marvelous, solid machine
Ah, but the look on the poor builder's face

Standing in mighty splendor there
Ready at last to perform
Produced with such meticulous care
But that builder's look of forlorn

An incredible sight, shiny sprockets and gears
Belts and pulleys percisely arranged
It had taken many painstaking years
But now, and this is the part most strange

The machine didn't work, didn't move one iota
The builder was quickly asked why
It runs on LOVE and we've exhausted our quota
Not enough to even beg, borrow or buy

His countenance becoming more than sad
His gnarled hands raised in dismay
He had given all he ever had
To celebrate this completion day

Alas, it was a frightful time, frightful and cruel
Mankind fighting itself it seemed
We saw it coming but somehow fooled
Yes, very real, not a horrible dream

We ran out of LOVE, forgot how to generate more
Only room in hearts for hate
Without LOVE his creation stuck to the floor
To rust and seize up it's ultimate fate

Where did the LOVE go? Did it simply disappear?
Why did it completely waste away?
Why??? We threw it away because of mistrust and fear
And we should have known it would happen one day

With LOVE lost, the end a real possibility
Nothing will function in a world of black hearts
If this is to become our new reality
Healing will have to immediately start

I decide to start this very day
Won't you join me in this endeavor?
For if we don't, LOVE will be gone to stay
The machine stuck to the floor forever

That Glance

a glance
yeah
that glance
burning through me
like the sun through a magnifying glass
brightly illuminating my imperfections
then burning it's way into my ability to forget them
because you won't
a glance
yeah
that glance
your weapon of choice
with which you are sure you'll win
change me
remake me
configure me
into your perception of who you think I should be
you will not win
i have found the shade
in which your glance cannot be magnified
her eyes
her eyes look straight at me
straight through my imperfections
into my heart
i will forever be sheltered from your glance
yeah
that glance

I Watched You Dance

I watched you dance
Joyful spinning, twirling
Your spirit shining
A light so wonderous bright
My heart drinking in that heady potion
Spinning, twirling in step with you
Ah!
I could but watch
My feet planted firmly in place
Yet
My heart your unseen partner
Joyful spinning, twirling
I watched you dance

It All Came to Me!

It ALL came to me!
In an instant
A brilliant, exhilarating, incredible instant
Suddenly, I see it clearly
In total
Crystal
Now
Now
It ALL makes sense
ALL of it
Amazing!
Nothing hidden
Nothing
Oh, how I have longed for this day
To see what but very, very few see
To understand that which only the enlightened understand
To know
Absolutely
To be granted this unimaginable privilege
It ALL came to me!
Finally
Finally
I too can become a color analyst on a sports telecast
Finally
It ALL came to me

It's Out There

It's out there
You know it is
How?
Look at the way they hold hands
Not just holding
But
Holding on
Like forever
It's out there
You know it is
How?
Because they kiss under the streetlight
To kiss yes
But
To show the world their kiss
It's out there
You know it is
How?
They look directly into each other's eyes
Looking
Looking
And
Smiling
It's out there
You know it is
How?
Their smiles communicate
In a way words cannot
They know
They surely know
What those smiles mean
It's out there
You know it is
Wish I did

Accepted, Loved, Liked

If you're begging for acceptance
Pleading your case endlessly
Same old song and dance
Wonder why you can't see

If you beg someone to love you
Even beg on your knees
If determined to see it through
What base instinct are you trying to please

If you demand others to like you
Say you'll drop them if they don't
What endless hurt are you getting into
Chances are they simply won't

Some lessons to be learned here
Not easy but there is no doubt
To me it wasn't always clear
But hope you'll hear me out

Plant acceptance, loving, liking
By example you'll be known
The results may prove striking
Getting back what you've sown

How do I know you may wonder
Do I believe I'm an authority
Is it just an impression I am under
Did my advice work for me

Yes, but not automatically
It's experience, learning from mistakes
I'm not saying it happens easily
Or estimating how long it should take

One cannot beg nor demand
A human heart to conform
It does not feel according to plans
Or only comply when warned

For acceptance try accepting
For love try loving first
To be liked stop rejecting
Quenching that for which you thirst

Oh, you are not obligated
To believe in what I say
I just want your desires satiated
Accepted, loved and liked today

Did You Ever?

Did you ever try to convince yourself
You were absolutely positive you would
But a situation came up unexpectedly
And you wondered if you really could

Did you ever see something you really wanted
Knew you just had to get
But circumstances dictated that
You couldn't get that thing just yet

Did you ever go that extra, super extra mile
Only to realize there were miles still to travel
Or get yourself wound up in something
You knew would take superhuman effort to unravel

Did you ever love that "one and only" love
But your love wasn't their "one and only"
Pain eventually turning to only numbness
The nothingness feeling of the lonely

Did you ever feel any of those things
I don't need to know, just wondered if it be
But I will tell you without hesitation
They were all "DID YOU EVER" to me

The More You Don't Know

The more you know
You realize
The more you don't know
The more you don't know
The more you want to know
The more you want to know
The more you know
The more you know
The more you don't know
Vicious cycle?
No!
Beautiful cycle
Get on it and ride!

Museum

Gonna open up an emporium
NO! NO!
Stuff's not for sale
A museum
That's it!
A museum
Where you can come in and see my collections
Maybe even a section for stuff I used to have
Put pictures there
Wait!
Can you take pictures of feelings, emotions, love?
Oh, oh
I'll put the words there
On big posters
The feeling words
Maybe even in frames
You know
Make em look nice
The stuff I used to have section
Yeah
Museum
Not ready yet
Close
Oh!
It'll be free
Everything I ever had I gave free
Won't need a big space
Biggest part'll be the stuff I used to have section
Yeah
A museum
Gonna open up a museum

I Know I Read It

Hey! I got your note
thanks
can't seem to find it now
but
I know I read it
read it three times
said you missed me
asked about my family
I got a little misty
thought you might want to hook up
you know, lunch
or, or
something
you didn't mention it
hope you're ok
hell
hope you're great!
jeez
wish I could find that note
I know I read it
after all this time
I, I
I know I wouldn't have tossed it
couldn't have just disappeared
I …. …!
I …. …!
oh, never mind
that's something I shouldn't say
I got your note
thanks
damn!
can't seem to find it now
I know I read it

Astride This Horse

How long astride this horse
Upon which you have no control
To stay the the desired course
Must you surrender the reins of your soul

Yes, you so wanted this steed
His flaming mane a symbol of change
But will his propensity to stampede
Cause your thought process to rearrange

Will you now at last try to rein him in
Or once this wild is there no recourse
Riding at great speed to the chasm's rim
Yet you continue astride this horse

Around The Table

There!
In that old farm house
Around the table
Ma, Pa, Billy, Suzy, Baby
Warm light shining on a glorious scene
I notice as I'm driving by
Suddenly. Without warning
A tear
Just one
Warm
Slowly sliding down my cheek
Eyes on the road
Heart in the past
A scene once prevalent
Almost extinct
Dinner meeting
Important meeting
Vital meeting
Family together
Around the table!

Trail Of Dreams

Gentle breeze as a caress
Breeze, yet something more I feel
This sense that I have just been blessed
An unseen kiss, could it be real?

Meandering on this trail of dreams
Through the wood of my memories
Hand in hand with her it seems
Ah foolish heart, could it truly be?

As these old feelings well up again
At last, at last, I'll not be alone
So close as I reach out and then
The nagging buzz of my chairside phone

Jolting me back to reality
To this desk at which a different scene
Perhaps one day it will really be
Now? Only on this trail of dreams

Damage Report

I might be able to use that
Think twice before you throw it away
It used to be mine as a matter of fact
Yes mine, prior to my yesterdays

You've made it clear that you don't intend to keep it
It has sustained some damage at your hand
I'll take it back although it may not fit
In the deepest part of this man

Be careful as you hand it to me
More damage I could not bear
I'm paying dearly for what I gave for free
Praying that with time it may begin to repair

Not sure that I could give it once more
This strong man made as one so weak
Who really knows what life has in store
Or exactly what it is I seek

I Need To Believe

I need to believe in Santa again
And
Frosty
The Easter Bunny
The Tooth Fairy
Because
If I can get to that place
That magical place
Then I can believe
That all children will remain safe
Religious wars will cease
All colors will be accepted
Celebrated
Appreciated
Worth will be measured by giving
Not
By getting
Ideas can be shared
Not scorned
Compromise
Blessed compromise will be fashionable
Music will play in each heart
I need to believe in Santa again

Perhaps

Perhaps a bachelor doesn't want to be
Seeing only that which he desires not to see
Perhaps the results of earlier seeds that were sown
Convincing him life is better on his own

Perhaps in the furthest recesses of his mind
He secretly wishes a better existence to find
Perhaps he needs to convince himself everyday
That for him, his way is the only way

Perhaps sometimes as the daylight fades
He struggles to justify mistakes that he's made
Perhaps that inner battle continues to rage
Until he surrenders and believes, "not at my age"

Perhaps there may be hope for my bachelor friend
After all, life isn't over until it ends
Perhaps his Angel will appear and he'll see
Just maybe a bachelor doesn't want to be

And Still I Wonder

And still I wonder
What life could be

I've rounded corners
Opened some doors
Been liked by some
Loved many more

Tamed my fears
Fulfilled some desires
Put out a few
And started other fires

And still I wonder
What life could be

I passed most tests
A couple were failed
I've laughed out loud
And silently wailed

Did good deeds
Perhaps some bad
No one can steal
The fun I've had

And still I wonder
What life could be

Got along with most
Called some brother
Disagreed with some
Fought with others

Voiced my opinion
Compromised when required
Landed good jobs
Yeah, once got fired

And still I wonder
What life could be

Yes, still I wonder
Is the answer above?
What life could be
Having real love

The love of a woman
A love never broken
When glances are as special
As all the words spoken

And still I wonder
What life could be

Maybe I'll find her
When least expected
And look back at this
Upon which I've reflected

And still I wonder
What life could be

Drifting

Drifting over a sea of flowers
There!
There it is!
The one I want
Ah, I can pick any but that one
That one is off limits
Illegal to pick
But
It's the one I want!
Oh
To be denied
Or
Pick it and suffer the consequences
Certain consequences
Floating toward trouble
Sweet trouble
Reaching
Awake!
Awake!
No flower
No consequences
Where will I drift tonight?

Empty

Why did you decide to dump it out?
Did you think it was getting stale?
It seemed to work so effectively
At what point did it start to fail?

Emptiness is a frightening feeling
Even more devastating than sad
For it results in numbness, nothingness
Losing every feeling one ever had

When feelings are absent, one is truly alone
Impervious to what new possibilities exist
They say time is a tonic, a refill if you will
Eventually one is unable to resist

Opening the refill, slowly beginning
To partake of it's refreshing, it's healing
Once again to believe in the miracle
Of discovering one's lost feelings

Bound With Blue

Begging for opportunity
To flash once more
My whole being trying to remember
What it used to flash for
But there is no reason
Since I lost you
My smile will forever
Be bound with blue

They touch but don't feel
Work but accomplish little
My whole being laments
One answer only to this riddle
That answer but a memory
It left with you
My hands will forever
Be bound with blue

It aches constantly
With a dull, hazy pain
My whole being seeks relief
Alas, there be no gain
No remedy exists
Apart from being with you
My mind will forever
Be bound with blue

Oh!!!! Set me free!
It cries from within
My whole being agrees
Yet knows not where to begin
For there will never be
Another such as you
My heart will forever
Be bound with blue

A Rush

There is a rush
People tripping over each other
Pushing, shoving
To claim their share
Maybe claiming more than a share
Mining more than a share
It's worth so much to them
Afflicted with need
Fever!
On they come
To the mother lode
Risking everything
Family
Friends
Even their sanity
To fill their pouches
To fill their minds
To fill their hearts
Mining misery
A rush

It Is Deafening

It is deafening
Permeating the mind
Sharp, piercing
Permeating the soul
As if by osmosis
A cacophony
Harsh, unrelenting
It is deafening
It surrounds
Rendering one
Unable to function
To reason
Scarcely to breath
It is deafening
Capturing sanity
Locking it away
Pain
Like no other
Why do others not hear?
It is deafening
This silence

Recycle

Recycle
Noble endeavor
Use what remains
Melt it down
Grind it
Pulverize it
Remold
Remake
But
Is there hope?
Will it work?
For
A heart?
My heart?

Beanstalks

Sold the cow for a handful of beans
What be the profit there you fool?
But beanstalks will grow if you sow
And beanstalks can be cool

Oh, I'm not saying you'll get rich
Like some fantastic tale
But beanstalks can turn a bit of profit
If the bean crop doesn't fail

There was a kid once name of Jack
Who did realize a tidy sum
Gold coins, golden egg and a lovely golden harp
Before his climbing days were done

Seems he had a bit o trouble with some big guy
And had to destroy the old beanstalk
Don't know if I completely buy that story
Think it's just some made up talk

Who knows, guess it could be true
Stranger things have happened, and so
I'm wishing you a handful of beans
And I hope the damn things grow!

Shoes

Don't walk a mile in my shoes
Walk a million miles beside me in yours
In my shoes
The journey has been mine
In your shoes
Yours
In our shoes
Ah, the possibilities!
Walk with me, talk with me
Do not echo me, pacify me, always agree with me
Let me know how you feel
How you would like to feel
How I can help you feel that
On our journey
In our shoes
Shoes!

Man in the Window

The man in the window motioned me
Come in son take a peek
Said if you like it in here boy
You can stay most of a week

Twenty years now gone by
Haven't even looked outside
I'm breathin, almost movin
But my insides are fried

I'm touchin only what keeps me here
But I ain't feelin a thing
All I gotta do is reach
Move my fingers, pull a string

I'm needin what's on the string
Need it more than I need air
Lord, if that man ever motions you
Don't slide your ass in here

Cause waste is all it's gonna mean
A waste of humankind
Yeah, guess I was a part of that
Til that first peek made me blind

Love? Don't think I know the word
Seems it's rattlin round somewhere
But how it feels, what it's like
I got nothin to compare

The man in the window laughin
Cause he getting all I got
Look, he sure ain't getting much
Might have nothin left, but damn I forgot

Must have a little, cause he keepin me
Reachin for the stuff
When my fingers pull that string no more
Is when I've had enough

Bury me without a prayer
Eulogy? A dust ball on the floor
And the man still be in the window
Motionin to bring in more

To take a peek, pull the string
Til they got no will to leave
And when they die, no one cares
Only dust balls left to grieve

But until then, the man suck them dry
Of their money, their hope, their heart
And my friends, though we have never met
That ain't the end, it's just the start

Cause new ones will be tempted
To come in and take a peek
The man in the window laughin
Cause they'll give him most of a week

The Box

I opened the box
It was me inside
How did I get there?
What made me decide?

To inhabit a place
With no room to grow
Stunted by perceptions
With seeds left to sow

Let me now cast
Seeds to the wind
To grow where they will
Their maturing begin

Perhaps when they ripen
Grown tall enough to see
I'll discover this box
Is too small for me

Midnight on the Water

Midnight on the water
Moonlit boat ride as if on glass
Planning this romantic adventure for months
The perfect night had come at last
By my side my lovely fiance
Even the one so hard to please
Muttering of her bent for seasickness
Whining that she was about to freeze
I stammered, but my darling
I acquired this vessel just for you
She replied tersely, yes, of course
Like the other inconsiderate things you do
She reminded, I have insisted since we met
You do nothing without my consent
I was getting more and more irritated
As further down the river we went
Her shrill voice rang out in the silent night
Turn this rickety tub around
My head taking on such an ache
Catching each and every decibel of the sound
But, sometimes plans do work out
As did this, bringing welcome relief
Thinking, now I must cancel our wedding arrangements
As my dear intended slipped beneath

Acknowledgements:

My mother Ethel Famoly who shared with me her love of "the written word."

My daughter Trista and my son Zachary who have always believed in me.

To the loves I have gained, the loves I have lost and the true love I have finally found.

Bruce Famoly is a lifelong resident of the Skaneateles, New York area. His interest in writing began when he was convinced to portray Scrooge in a comedy version of *A Christmas Carol*. Upon hearing the raucous laughter of the audience as he delivered his first line, he became immediately hooked on "the arts." When Bruce was asked to do other short plays and to M.C. Charity events he became convinced that he had things to say that others may be interested in. Bruce began writing in earnest in 2001 when he submitted a short piece to the local newspaper and was asked by the editor to submit more, beginning a weekly column called "Famoly Forum." Writing poetry soon followed and poetry became Bruce's primary focus and he considers it a form of therapy. Bruce has also writes song lyrics and enjoys the process of writing as much at the final result.

www.ingramcontent.com/pod-product-compliance
Lightning Source LLC
Chambersburg PA
CBHW052121110526
44592CB00013B/1698